She is Me

j.
iron word

www.jironword.com

Instagram @j.ironword

Facebook J. Iron Word

Twitter @JIronword

Cover designed by Jonathan W. Myers

For you Queen

Chapter

1

Her

She is

**She is a ripped jean
wearing, cussword
swearing, lightning
bolt in human form,
with a heart that
could melt the Sun.**

8-23-2019 / j. iron word

Once in a Lifetime

She's a balance of strength
and femininity. She's a blend
of silly and serious. She's a
dreamer with her feet still on
the ground. She is the kind of
person that can find the suns
rays in a rainstorm. She is a once
in a lifetime woman.

8-15-2019 / j. iron word

Heartbeat

She finds her heartbeat in the things that have no heartbeat at all, like the sun, the moon, the ocean and its sand.

9-11-2018 / j. iron word

Sky Depth

She has a thing for deep conversations and cotton candy skies.

8-18-2019 / j. iron word

Growing Pains

She is tired more days than not, but she is growing more days than not too and that growth is her secret weapon.

7-28-2018 / j. iron word

Wildly

**She owned her curves,
the way a tiger owns
the jungle**

wildly.

4-22-2019 / j. iron word

Dear Queen,

I like your rebellious ways and
the fact that your heart and
mind can never fit into any box,
because you are uniquely you.

Love always,

j. iron word / 8-20-2018

Stand tall

In a world of copycats, she was unique and stood out because she was perfectly happy being imperfectly herself.

2-25-2019 / j. iron word

Chaotic

**At first glance she's
a mess, but a deeper dive into
the woman that she is will show
you she's the most chaotically
organized human you have ever
met.**

9-30-2018 / j. iron word

Deserving

I hope whoever gets to call you baby, loves you like a *Queen*.

2-28-2019 / j. iron word

Greatness

**Most days she is up working,
before the sun has even moved
a muscle.**

**She knows if she wants to be
great, she cannot settle for
mediocrity in herself.**

4-9-2019 / j. iron word

Most Days

She doesn't always crave candlelight; most days she is a ponytail, wine and pizza kind of girl.

8-10-2018 / j. iron word

Action

Instead of making excuses, she makes things happen.

She is a human of action.

8-7-2019 / j. iron word

Self-made

**She was born
a beautiful soul,
but she's a
self-made badass.**

8-3-2019 / j. iron word

Incredible

**She is far from perfect,
but free in spirit and wild in
heart.**

She is imperfectly incredible.

8-3-2019 / j. iron word

Balanced

**She is a balance of beauty,
soul, sexy and intellect,
otherworldly on every level.**

8-2-2019 / j. iron word

Not Even

**There is no
quit in her,
not even in
her tired.**

12-17-2017 / j. iron word

Calligraphy

**In a world of emojis,
she is calligraphy.**

2-18-2019 / j. iron word

Little Bit

**She will always
have a little bit of
gangster under
her crown.**

7-30-2019 / j. iron word

Wildling

**She's a wild thing,
with a soft heart and
deep mind.**

11-3-2018 / j. iron word

Utterly

You are beautiful for reasons that have nothing to do with your physical beauty, while still being utterly gorgeous.

7-24-2019 / j. iron word

Goddess

**You are a Goddess,
fuck anyone who
makes you think
anything less.**

2-9-2019 / j. iron word

Optimist

**She finds beauty in clouds
and treasure in trash. She
knows there is a great deal
of amazing in the broken
and misunderstood.**

**She has learned from
rainstorms. She is priceless
even though others have
discarded her.**

**It is not what others think
that matters, but what she
knows to be true.**

1-30-2019 / j. iron word

Everything

**She's a little bit
of everything you
could ever ask for
in a human.**

10-14-2018 / j. iron word

Complex Beauty

**You could take away the filters
and the angles, the fancy
captions and the hash tags and
you will still be left with the
most beautifully complex
woman you have ever met.**

9-3-2018 / j. iron word

Shines

**Sometimes she's a sparkler,
other times she's a firework,
but no matter what she always
fucking shines.**

7-9-2019 / j. iron word

Bombshell

She's a beauty and a beast
wrapped into one bombshell
of a human. Conquering life
when others would have quit,
proving the doubters wrong
one goal at a time.

4-17-2019 / j. iron word

Unstoppable

She's unstoppable, even in her mismatched socks, yoga pants and ponytail.

She knows it's not what she wears, but how she wears it.

2-19-2015 / j. iron word

Chaotic Moon

**She can be as calm as a
full moon, but her soul will
always be a little rock and roll.**

6-21-2019 / j. iron word

Growth

She is the truth,
authentic, real,
a constant work
in progress of
beautiful imperfection.
Never doing things
because "she said,"
or "he said," rather
because she herself
wants to; because her
soul needs to.

1-16-2019 / j. iron word

Answered Prayer

**She will never be a saint,
but she will always be the
fallen angel you pray for.**

6-13-2019 / j. iron word

Diamond

While she is as hard as a diamonds edge, she is soft when it matters most, with who matters most.

6-13-19 / j. iron word

Yin-Yang

**She's a rebel
with an old soul
and a pure heart.**

7-23-18 / j. iron word

Appreciation

**She has an appreciation
for art and architecture,
history and souls, love and
other things that seem to be
overlooked by the modern
human.**

12-26-2018 / j. iron word

Ever

**She is the
sweetest badass
you will ever meet.**

12-20-2017 / j. iron word

Fool

**Anyone who judges her
is a fool. She is living life
as it should be lived,**

on her own terms.

3-24-2019 / j. iron word

Life

Some mornings she
hid a little bit longer.

'The world could wait
for a few extra minutes,"
she thought.

As she buried her head
beneath her pillows the
sun peeked in just enough
to remind her that *life was
beautiful*.

    11-5-2018 / j. iron word

Indestructible

She may not always
feel invincible, but
at the end of the day
she is indestructible.

11-1-2018 / j. iron word

Wonder Woman

**She's the kind of
woman that will make
you wonder where she
has been your whole
life.**

10-27-2018 / j. iron word

Again

**She's an angel, but not
because she's perfect or
because she can fly, rather
because she fell and flew
again.**

9-11-2018 / j. iron word

Destination Her

**She smiles as she
remembers where
she came from, where
she is and where she
is going.**

11-17-2017 / j. iron word

Art

**If you were to draw
her she would be all heart,
because she is love in human
form.**

5-13-2019 / j. iron word

Wisdom

When my daughter was 11 her friend was sad on her own birthday. She wanted to tell her crush that she liked him, but when he found out, he was rude to her and it made her cry.

My daughter told her, *"Don't worry about him, you don't need a guy like that."*

Reminder to all the Queens out there who have tear stained cheeks because of a man.

"You don't need a guy like that."

1-22-2019 / j. iron word

Always

Being beautiful is easy, but her kind of beautiful is rare and exotic.

She is beautiful that is as luminous on the inside as she is on the outside.

3-11-2019 / j. iron word

Dangerous

**She's dangerous,
because she knows
what she's capable of.**

12-30-2018 / j. iron word

That Kind

**She's the kind
of beautiful that
can make a grown
man nervous.**

11-9-2018 / j. iron word

Depth

**She has a smile
that tells you her soul
is nothing but beautiful beneath
her skin.**

11-7-2018 / j. iron word

If she

If she looks back,
it is only to see how
far she has come and
how much she has
grown.

11-5-2018 / j. iron word

Anything

**They say get a girl
that can do both, but
she is a woman who
can do anything.**

10-15-2018 / j. iron word

Her Presence

**There was a beautiful to her
that no camera could ever catch,
an energy and warmth that
could only be felt in her
presence.**

8-18-2018 / j. iron word

Vintage

In a world of scrolling screens,
she still has an appreciation for
ink and paper between her
fingertips.

8-13-2018 / j. iron word

Independent

**She is not the type to depend
on others, she relies most on
the feathers of her own wings.**

10-3-2018 / j. iron word

Flutter

**She could have been born
a butterfly, but at the last
minute God made her a woman.**

**The universe needed her
amazing to last longer than
a flutter.**

4-4-2019 / j. iron word

Slay

**Once she learned
she was incomparable,
there was no stopping her, life
was hers to slay.**

3-28-2019 / j. iron word

Extra

**She is what some may call a
"little extra," but what else
would you expect from a limited
edition *Queen*.**

3-20-2019 / j. iron word

Mother

You are a creator of the
universe. You raise the
future of our planet. You
teach humans to love and
show us the meaning of the
word unconditional. You make
sacrifice seem as commonplace
as breathing. You open our eyes
to our dreams and let us know
that they can become our
reality. You are a living
illustration of strength.
Without you, there would
be no me.

5-11-2019 / j. iron word

Chapter

2

Loving Her

High Maintenance

**She is the kind of high
maintenance that seems to
be too much for the modern
man; craving the most priceless
of things, conversations that
last until the sun rises, a lifetime
of memories and unconditional
love to name a few.**

10-30-2018 / j. iron word

Soul Lyrical

If you want to understand her soul, listen, especially in the lyrics that she sings and the music that she jams.

8-20-2019 / j. iron word

Inside Out

She wants be to be called
beautiful by the human that
loves her from her soul to her
sense of humor, from her laugh
to the tears that on occasion
find her cheeks, from the tips of
her fingers to the depth of her
heart.

What she needs is to be called
beautiful by the person who
knows her inside and out and
loves her because of it.

4-15-2019 / j. iron word

Worth

**She has been there and done
that, she knows her worth and
what she deserves. She wouldn't
sell herself short for anything
less than everything.**

5-9-2019 / j. iron word

Reminded

**She does not care to be every
human's desire, but she does
need to be reminded she is your
only desire.**

2-16-2019 / j. iron word

Effort

**She is something of a
mystery and hopes to
be never fully understood,
but she does desire the
sincere effort of a soul
trying to.**

1-8-2019 / j. iron word

Chosen

**The soul that wins her
heart will be the one who is
patient and understanding
enough to wait out her walls.**

6-6-2019 / j. iron word

#1

**Make sure to lift her up
on the days when she needs it,
but also on the days when she is
already on top of the world.**

**She needs to be reminded that
you are always her number one
fan.**

4-28-2019 / j. iron word

Listen and Learn

**A mind like hers
should be listened to
and learned from.**

4-28-2019 / j. iron word

All Days

Love her, not just on the good days, but all days, and on the days she needs more, be more, be her everything.

8-8- 2019 / j. iron word

Ocean

**Like the ocean she is life.
She has depths that will
never be fully discovered,
her love is always present
and her emotions come in
waves.**

7-29-2018 / j. iron word

Multidimensional

There are many sides to her,
facets of her that exist. Most
however, will never see or know
those versions of her. But the
truth is most are undeserving, as
knowing all of her is a privilege
that must be earned.

8-9-2019 / j. iron word

Fearless Love

Don't be afraid to grab her and kiss her like your hearts next beat depended on it, reminding her of the passion behind your love.

8-1-2018 / j. iron word

Borderless

**She's the kind of woman
that will make you wish borders
didn't exist and distance was
only a state of mind.**

4-1-2019 / j. iron word

Gone Girl

A woman like her
can't be missed when she
walks into a room, but you
are guaranteed to miss her
long after she is gone.

3-28-2019 / j. iron word

Better

**If she's screaming,
it's because she cares.**

**If she's crying, it's
because she hurts.**

**If she's gone, it's
because she knew
she deserved better.**

12-3-2018 / j. iron word

Naked Soul

Take the time to talk to her, the
time to get to know her. Stop
and listen to not only what she
is saying, but even more so to
what she is not. Do not be afraid
of being vulnerable with her,
because she is worthy of your
naked soul.

6-30-2018 / j. iron word

Someone's Queen

Be with a human that memorizes the shape of your earlobe, the curve in your chin and the dimples in your knees, once you find this human you will know what it means to be someone's Queen.

4-9-2018 / j. iron word

Chapter

3

Truth

A Look

Someone once asked me
how do you know if someone
loves you and I told them it's in
the way they look at you.

A look that says they would
hold back the ocean for you if
they could.

8-28-2018 / j. iron word

Over and Over

**Be with the
one who gives you
"the best day ever,"
over and over
again.**

6-16-2018 / j. iron word

Cravings

**More than sex,
I crave affection;
I need to feel loved.**

9-10-2015 / j. iron word

Details

**Find someone who will pay
attention to your details and
love you completely for them.**

3-16-2019 / j. iron word

Old Friend

The moon and I are on a first name basis, after keeping each other company on our quietest nights.

3-14-2019 / j. iron word

Unspoken

What I cannot articulate in words I show in emotions, listen to the sound of my actions to understand my heart.

4-23-2019 / j. iron word

Both

**My heart is both my
greatest weakness
and my superpower.**

12-15-2017 / j. iron word

Unshaken

**There is something to
be said about a person who
does not allow negativity
to overtake their soul, no matter
how many rainy days their heart
has known.**

3-20-2019 / j. iron word

Worth the Wait

**I am waiting, for someone to
sink their teeth into my soul,
dig their nails into my mind
and moan to the rhythm of
my hearts beat.**

3-6-2019 / j. iron word

Light

One day someone will see the light pouring through your cracks and love you more for each beam.

3-1-2019 / j. iron word

Soul Growing

**Sometimes tears
need to fall to water
the earth beneath
your soul.**

1-17-2019 / j. iron word

Soul Smile

The older you get the less you chase people and the more you chase moments that make your soul smile.

2-21-2018 / j. iron word

Vision

**My eyes are not
what they used to
be, they no longer
look at people's
appearance, but
how they are and
how they treat
others.**

5-8-2019 / j. iron word

Wanted

I want the kind of love
that includes date nights
to Target and Starbucks. I
want the kind of love that
celebrates family members
birthdays and holidays together.
I want the kind of love that
includes Chinese takeout at
home and Netflix cuddles. I
want the kind of love that craves
rainy Sundays and pushes me on
sluggish Mondays. I want the
kind of love that can't be found
on the pages of the internet, but
that lives and breathes in real
life.

8-4-2019 / j. iron word

Complicated

I am most at peace in the
company of none, but there is a
select few of hand picked souls
that know my wild, crazy and
quirky. To those on the outside
looking in I will seem like a
complicated mess. But to the
ones that know me best, I will
always be more simple and than
the rest, preferring things that
come with a price tag of my
trust.

7-21-2019 / j. iron word

Hungry

I don't want a "complete"
person. I want someone
like me.

Someone who is
always trying to be a
better version of
themselves.

Not because I or anyone
else asked them to be, but
because it is a natural drive
from within.

Someone with an unrelenting
hunger for more, to be more.

3-26-2019 / j. iron word

Tunnel Vision

**Our physical appearance
is the smallest part of us,
but somehow it is all people see.**

1-19-2017 / j. iron word

One Love

Saying "I love you" is easy,
but there is a hard part of love,
the staying part, when others
would walk away; the part of
love that takes compromise &
communication. Then there is
the part of love that takes
patience and understanding.
No one has ever said love is
easy, but there is nothing more
powerful that two hearts
working on one love together.

3-28-2019 / j. iron word

Determined

**Even the longest and most
broken roads do not stand a
chance against the bare feet
of a determined soul.**

12-4-2017 / j. iron word

All Right

**All the wrong ones
will lead you to the
only right one.**

6-1-2019 / j. iron word

Only

**You can only love
someone as much
as their walls allow
you to.**

3-23-2019 / j. iron word

That Kind

I want a love that includes
sunsets and sunrises, the kind
that you're grateful for at the
end of the day and wake up
excited about. A goodnight and
good morning baby kind of
love.

7-26-2018 / j. iron word

Others

**Some people will love
you until they have
gotten their "use" out
of you, others will love
you until they have used
their last heartbeat
loving you.**

5-21-2019 / j. iron word

Hands On

**What we crave most
is a best friend, that
we can't keep our
hands off of.**

11-24-2016 / j. iron word

Balance

**I need a balance
of independence
and soul smothering
love.**

11-16-2019 / j. iron word

Gift

**Sometimes the best gift
you could receive from
someone is for them to
be present.**

(And Vice Versa)

12-27-2018 / j. iron word

The Excuse

Instead of settling for someone who gives you excuses, be with someone who makes you the excuse.

1-25-2019 / j. iron word

Goodbyes

If you believe in love, you also have to learn to believe in goodbyes.

11-6-2018 / j. iron word

Excite Me

**If you can't excite
my soul, you can't
excite my body.**

5-20-2019 / j. iron word

Savagely

**We live in a world where
everyone wants to be a savage,
but all we really want is to love
and be loved savagely.**

5-20-2019 / j. iron word

Understood

**I don't want someone
who tells me to calm
down.**

**What I need is someone to
listen to me and understand
why I am frustrated.**

10-8-2018 / j. iron word

Miss Me

**The very same people
who take you for granted
are the ones that miss you
the most when you're gone.**

12-16-2018 / j. iron word

Fixable

**And sometimes
love is going back
to a broken home
to fix it together.**

7-13-2018 / j. iron word

My why

**I am more silly than serious,
more quiet than loud, more
lover than fighter, but I will
fight for what I love.**

3-10-2019 / j. iron word

Custom Made

The words of affirmation you craved to hear from one but never did, will be sung to you often by the soul that was made to love you.

9-11-2018 / j. iron word

Real

**I miss you and I miss us,
not because we were perfect
or meant to be, but because
we were real.**

5-14-2019 / j. iron word

"Us"

I don't want greener grass.
I need love, loyalty, respect and
someone who is willing to fight
for "us" as hard as I am.

4-5-2019 / j. iron word

Worthy

You are worthy of
being listened to and heard.

You are worthy of being
respected and appreciated.

You *are* worthy of being missed
and dreamt about.

You are worthy of being loved
and adored.

You are worthy of being craved
and cared for. You are *worthy*.

11-8-2018 / j. iron word

Life Lessons

I have learned more about myself when I was falling apart, than when I had it together.

11-23-2018 / j. iron word

Priceless

We all fight silent battles, but do not talk about them.

If you are facing something and feel like it's no longer worth living, talk about it.

You are not alone.

Your life is priceless.

9-2-2018 / j. iron word

Alive

Some loves, the truest
of them, will touch parts of you
that you did not know existed
and reawaken parts of you that
you thought
were forever lost.

8-31-2018 / j. iron word

No settling

Don't ever be the one someone settled for, be the one they feel like they cannot live without.

5-29-2018 / j. iron word

Seen

**Maybe not every star
is meant to be seen by the
world. Maybe some stars
are only supposed to be
seen by their soul mates.**

8-11-2018 / j. iron word

Irreplaceable

**At the end of the day
we all want to be in love
with someone who is
afraid to lose us.**

8-7-2018 / j. iron word

Sabotage

You can love someone with everything you are and be everything they wanted and they will still sabotage the relationship. Don't blame yourself for other people's actions against your heart; their loss will be your gain in time.

9-15-2018 / j. iron word

All Along

One day all the broken pieces from your past will fall into place in the form of a heart that was beating for you all along.

9-15-2018 / j. iron word

Chapter

4

Love

Team

One plus one isn't one. I don't
need someone to complete me.
What I need is someone who
makes me a part of a two. A part
of a team that includes "me and
you."

2-5-2019 / j. iron word

Becoming

**You are becoming a
part of my good mornings and
goodnights, and in between I
find happiness in knowing your
heart exists and is somewhere
beating.**

4-30-2019 / j. iron word

Free

**I am free with you,
in all the ways I was
afraid to be with others.**

10-14-2018 / j. iron word

Never Alone

**I promise to listen
when you need to share
what's weighing on your
mind, and to be there when
you are not in the mood to
talk about it, but need to be
reminded that you are not
alone.**

5-6-2019 / j. iron word

Timeless

I want you to be more than a moment in my life's timeline.

I want you to be a million different moments that fill my forever.

10-23-2018 / j. iron word

Always

**Some days she's my muse,
others she's my frustration,
but no matter what she is
always my love.**

7-25-2019 / j. iron word

Beautiful Mind

"You make me nervous."

"Why nervous?"

"Because your physical beauty matches your mind's beauty."

"And how is my mind's beauty?"

"Endless"

1-28-2019 / j. iron word

Fun

**We have fun together,
the kind that makes other
people who see us smile.**

12-21-2018 / j. iron word

Fiercely

**While love is not a competition,
I want to make sure no other
soul could love you as fiercely as
I do.**

1-23-2019 / j. iron word

Help

"I need your help."

"Help with what?"

*"With writing your
half of our love
story."*

1-22-2019 / j. iron word

Where I Should Be

**If my heart had a compass
it would spin wildly when you
are near, telling me there was
nowhere else I should be than
beside you.**

1-17-2019 / j. iron word

Just Me

"I am just me," she said
and he knew she was right,
she was in fact just her.

A her was more rare than
one in 1 billion, more rare
than once in a lifetime.

She was a once in the
history of humanity
type of soul.

1-16-2019 / j. iron word

Heavy Lifting

**If I could carry your heavy heart
I would, but since I cannot just
know I am here for you in every
way you will allow me to be.**

1-8-2019 / j. iron word

Total

**In a world with so
much uncertainty.
At the end of the day
I want you to know
I love you, with
complete and
total certainty.**

1-11-2019 / j. iron word

Anything

**You can tell me anything
at any time. It's okay to be
human and have frustrations
and to voice them. I adore you
for your real and your raw, the
human that no one else knows
or sees, but me.**

10-21-2018 / j. iron word

Me

**I have never been
more me, than who
I am with you.**

5-18-2018 / j. iron word

No Distractions

**I want to love you
in an old school kind
of way, when the
only distraction
between two hearts
was the moon.**

12-6-2018 / j. iron word

Your Reason

I want to be the reason your heart believes in the magic of love.

9-18-2018 / j. iron word

Extraordinary

I want to worship you,
make you laugh,
make love to you.

Play with your hair
and caress your skin.

Get you water when you
are thirsty and be your
heater when you are cold.

I want to spend my days
reminding you that you
are loved and extraordinary.

4-11-2018 / j. iron word

Endlessly

**I want to kiss you endlessly
with the hope that we would
end up each other's forever.**

10-24-2018 / j. iron word

Stubborn Love

**She was born stubborn
but I'll take her stubborn
love over anyone's easy
going anything.**

10-23-2018 / j. iron word

Crave

**I crave your everything,
from your moods, to your skin,
your ideas, to your laughter,
your bad days, to your best
I crave you whole.**

9-30-2019 / j. iron word

Wild

He loved her for her sweet and her nurturing, but he craved her for her wild.

9-3-2018 / j. iron word

Back to Back

**From our beginning
until my end, I hope to
love you enough for two
lifetimes.**

5-19-2019 / j. iron word

Everywhere

**It's in the car ride conversations
with a destination to anywhere,
that take my heart everywhere
it's ever wanted to go with you.**

2-2-2018 / j. iron word

Fruition

**While I could paint you
with my eyes closed, I no
longer have to, because I
am lucky enough to love you
throughout my days and
my dreams.**

11-11-2017 / j. iron word

<u>Index</u>

Chapter 1
She is Me

She is	1
Once in a Lifetime	2
Heartbeat	3
Sky Depth	4
Growing Pains	5
Wildly	6
Dear Queen	7
Stand Tall	8
Chaotic	9
Deserving	10
Greatness	11
Most Days	12
Action	13
Self-Made	14
Incredible	15
Balanced	16
Not Even	17
Calligraphy	18
Little Bit	19
Wildling	20
Utterly	21
Goddess	22
Optimist	23
Everything	24
Complex Beauty	25
Shines	26
Bombshell	27
Unstoppable	28
Chaotic Moon	29
Growth	30
Answered Prayer	31
Diamond	32
Yin-Yang	33

Appreciation   34
Ever   35
Fool   36
Life   37
Indestructible   38
Wonder Woman   39
Again   40
Destination Her   41
Art   42
Wisdom   43
Always   44
Dangerous   45
That Kind   46
Depth   47
If She   48
Anything   49
Her Presence   50
Vintage   51
Independent   52
Flutter   53
Slay   54
Extra   55
Mother   56
Chapter 2 Loving Her   57
High Maintenance   59
Soul Lyrical   60
Inside out   61
Worth   62
Reminded   63
Effort   64
Chosen   65
#1   66
Listen and Learn   67
All Days   68
Ocean   69
Multidimensional   70
Fearless Love   71

Borderless   72
Gone Girl   73
Better   74
Naked Soul   75
Someone's Queen   76
Chapter 3 Truth   77
A Look   79
Over and Over   80
Cravings   81
Details   82
Old Friend   83
Unspoken   84
Both   85
Unshaken   86
Worth the Wait   87
Light   88
Soul Growing   89
Soul Smile   90
Vision   91
Wanted   92
Complicated   93
Hungry   94
Tunnel Vision   95
One Love   96
Determined   97
All Right   98
Only   99
That Kind   100
Others   101
Hands On   102
Balance   103
Gift   104
The Excuse   105

Goodbyes   106
Excite Me   107
Savagely   108
Understood   109
Miss Me   110
Fixable   111
My Why   112
Custom Made   113
Real   114
"Us"   115
Worthy   116
Life Lessons   117
Priceless   118
Alive   119
No Settling   120
Seen   121
Irreplaceable   122
Sabotage   123
All Along   124
Chapter 4 Love   125
Team   127
Becoming   128
Free   129
Never Alone   130
Timeless   131
Always   132
Beautiful Mind   133
Fun   134
Fiercely   135
Help   136
Where I Should Be   137
Just Me   138
Heavy Lifting   139
Total   140

Anything	141
Me	142
No Distractions	143
Your Reason	144
Extraordinary	145
Endlessly	146
Stubborn Love	147
Crave	148
Wild	149
Back to Back	150
Everywhere	151
Fruition	152

CPSIA information can be obtained
at www.ICGtesting.com
Printed in the USA
FSHW020339120520
69895FS